THE STORY OF THE
**NEW YORK
YANKEES**

Published by Creative Education
P.O. Box 227, Mankato, Minnesota 56002
Creative Education is an imprint of The Creative Company

Design and production by Blue Design
Printed in the United States of America

Photographs by Getty Images (Al Bello, Paul Cunningham/MLB Photos, Diamond Images, Focus on Sport, Jed Jacobsohn/ALLSPORT, Keystone, Kidwiler Collection/Diamond Images, Edwin Levick/Hulton Archive, Jim McIsaac, MLB Photos, Ralph Morse//Time Life Pictures, National Baseball Hall of Fame Library/MLB Photos, Hy Peskin/Time Life Pictures, Photo File/MLB Photos, Rich Pilling/MLB Photos, Louis Requena/MLB Photos, Arthur Rickerby/Diamond Images, Robert Riger, Mark Rucker/Transcendental Graphics, Jamie Squire, Mario Tama, MIKE THEILER/AFP)

Library of Congress Cataloging-in-Publication Data

Goodman, Michael E.
The story of the New York Yankees / by Michael Goodman.
p. cm.— (Baseball: the great American game)
Includes index.
ISBN-13: 978-1-58341-495-8
1. New York Yankees (Baseball team)—History—Juvenile literature. I. Title. II. Series.

GV875.N4G66 2007
796.357'64097471—dc22   2006027468

9 8 7 6 5 4 3 2

Cover: Outfielder Mickey Mantle
Page 1: Outfielder Joe DiMaggio
Page 3: Outfielder Hideki Matsui

THE STORY OF THE
NEW YORK YANKEES

by Michael E. Goodman

REGGIE JACKSON

THE STORY OF THE
New York Yankees

A buzz swirls through Yankee Stadium during the eighth inning of Game 6 of the 1977 World Series between the New York Yankees and Los Angeles Dodgers. "Can he do it again?" 55,000 fans ask each other. "He" is Yankees clean-up hitter Reggie Jackson. In his last two at bats, the slugging outfielder has jumped on the first pitch each time and slammed two-run homers into the right-field stands. Those four runs have put the Yankees in front, 4–3, and on the verge of winning the series. As Jackson approaches the plate in the eighth, the crowd begins to chant, "REG-GIE! REG-GIE! REG-

GIE!" Jackson steps in against Dodgers knuckleball pitcher Charlie Hough. Wasting no time, he attacks Hough's first fluttering delivery and sends it deep into the black-painted area beyond the center-field wall as the stadium erupts. Reggie Jackson has just faced three pitches, hit three home runs, and led the mighty Yankees to their 20th world championship.

NEW LEAGUE, NEW TEAM

Everything about New York City is big and exciting—from the skyscrapers that dominate the city's skyline, to the bright lights of its theaters along Broadway, to the fast-paced trading that goes on in the stock exchanges on Wall Street. New York is at the center of business, culture, and entertainment in the United States. Since 1903, New York has also been the home of the most successful sports franchise in American history—the New York Yankees.

The Yankees got their start in 1903 as one of the first teams in baseball's new American League (AL). The club was called the Highlanders then because it played its games at Hilltop Park, which sat on one of the highest points in New York. Because "Highlanders" took up too much space in newspaper headlines, however, local reporters began calling them the "Yankees." That name was made official in 1913.

In the Highlanders' first game in 1903, former Pittsburgh Pirates pitcher Jack Chesbro led the charge. He would have the best year of his career in 1904, though,

JACK CHESBRO – "Happy Jack" was the New York franchise's first star, a hurler famous for his spitball (a pitch that was legal in baseball's early years). His 41 victories in 1904 is a big-league record that will almost certainly stand forever.

NEW YORK CITY – The lights always seem to shine brighter in "The Big Apple." Throughout their history, the Yankees have received more publicity and coverage than perhaps any other major-league team, much of it earned by their success.

BABE RUTH

THE BABE CALLS HIS SHOT

Babe Ruth's feats on the ballfield inspired legends. One of the most famous involves an at bat during Game 3 of the 1932 World Series against the Chicago Cubs. As the game began, Chicago players and fans screamed at Ruth, calling him fat and washed-up. Ruth temporarily silenced them in the first inning when he smacked a pitch by Cubs hurler Charlie Root into the right-field stands to put the Yankees ahead, 3–0. In the fourth inning, when the Babe botched a play in right field that allowed Chicago to tie the game, the fans were ecstatic.

The catcalls grew louder when Ruth came to bat in the fifth. Ruth took two strikes; then he stuck out his arm and pointed. Was he pointing toward the pitcher, toward the Cubs dugout, or toward the center-field stands? No one is quite sure. But Ruth smashed the next pitch over the fence in the general direction in which he had been pointing. The next day, New York reporters wrote that Ruth had "called his shot," showing where he would hit the pitch. Because the story involved the Babe, most fans believed it happened just that way.

when he set a record for games won (41) that has stood ever since. In their early history, the Yankees were an up-and-down team—but mostly down. The club finished below .500 nine times between 1907 and 1918. Finally, in 1918, feisty manager Miller Huggins took over and rebuilt his team around powerful hitting, resulting in a 1919 club that led the AL with 45 home runs. That same year, slugging right fielder Babe Ruth of the Boston Red Sox hit 29 homers all by himself, and Huggins convinced Yankees owner Colonel Jacob Ruppert to obtain Ruth for New York. When Ruth hit 54 home runs for the 1920 Yankees, he not only set new club and league records, but he also out-homered nearly every other *team* in baseball!

Before Ruth came along, players hit home runs almost by accident. But the Babe swung from his heels, looking to blast the ball out of the park. He put so much effort into his swing that fans were thrilled even if he missed. When he connected, however, the effect on the crowd was almost magical. Newspaper reporters invented a new adjective to describe one of his majestic blasts: "Ruthian."

With Ruth on board, the Yankees decided to build a state-of-the-art stadium in the Bronx with dimensions that would fit the left-handed batter's skills. On opening day in 1923, Yankee Stadium, with its right-field fence then only 295 feet from home plate, welcomed 74,000 enthusiastic Yankees fans. The fans' excitement reached a fever pitch when Ruth smacked a home run to right to win the game. Yankee Stadium soon became known as "The House That Ruth Built."

Ruth was joined in 1923 by another superstar: first baseman Lou Gehrig. The two men were the key components of a dominant lineup that became known as

"Murderers' Row," and right behind them in the batting order were outfielder Bob Meusel and second baseman Tony Lazzeri. The sluggers of Murderers' Row claimed their first world championship in 1923. That was followed by titles in 1927, 1928, and 1932. After Ruth retired in 1934, Gehrig starred on four more Yankees championship teams during the 1930s.

If Ruth was spectacular, Gehrig was steady. "He could hit a ball harder in every direction than any man who ever played," said Yankees catcher Bill Dickey. Even more impressive than Gehrig's hitting was his durability. Between June 1, 1925, and May 1, 1939, Gehrig played in 2,130 consecutive contests, a record that lasted until Baltimore Orioles shortstop Cal Ripken Jr. surpassed it in 1995. What finally stopped his streak was an incurable muscle disease called amyotrophic lateral sclerosis (ALS), which stole his strength and, in 1941, took his life. ALS is still known as "Lou Gehrig's Disease."

THE STREAK

During the summer of 1941, Americans' minds were focused on two subjects: what Adolf Hitler's army was doing in Europe and whether Joe DiMaggio's hitting streak was still going strong. Starting on May 15, the center fielder recorded at least one hit every game for two months, for 56 games in all. (Previously, the longest streak had been 41 games, by first baseman George Sisler of the St. Louis Browns in 1922.) According to an article in *Time* magazine, "In 102 years of baseball, few feats have caused such nationwide to-do. Joe's hits have been the biggest news in U.S. sport." Even radio programs were interrupted to announce that DiMaggio had just gotten a hit. DiMaggio had a few close calls during the streak, sometimes failing to get a hit until his last at bat. Although the pressure was intense, "Joltin' Joe" always seemed composed on the outside. "But that doesn't mean I wasn't dying inside," he later confided to reporters. The streak finally ended on July 17 in Cleveland against the Indians. During those 56 games, DiMaggio batted a remarkable .408 with 15 homers. More importantly, the Yankees' record during the streak was 44–12, and they soon captured another AL pennant.

CENTERS OF ATTENTION

ear the end of Gehrig's career, center fielder Joe DiMaggio arrived in New York. The quiet DiMaggio led his teammates more by example than by emotion. "He did things so easily," commented catcher Bill Dickey, "people didn't realize how good he was." DiMaggio conducted himself with such grace on and off the field that reporters began calling him "The Yankee Clipper" after the elegant sailing ships.

DiMaggio's career in New York lasted only 13 years, but during that time, the Yanks won an incredible 11 pennants and 10 World Series. DiMaggio twice topped the AL in home runs, won two batting titles, and captured three Most Valuable Player (MVP) awards—all impressive feats. But what he accomplished in 1941 was truly remarkable. That season, Joltin' Joe recorded at least one hit in 56 consecutive games, a record no other major-league player has come close to equaling. "The 1941 streak was an unbelievable thing—day after day," recalled Yankees Hall of Fame shortstop Phil Rizzuto. "I don't think he got a soft hit the entire 56 games."

With DiMaggio leading the way, the Yankees seemed invincible throughout the 1940s and into the next decade. The club set a major-league record by winning five straight championships between 1949 and 1953 and continued

PITCHER · WHITEY FORD

Edward "Whitey" Ford dominated AL batters with guile rather than power. He could deliver any of four pitches—fastball, slider, curve, or sinker—from a variety of arm angles, so a hitter never knew just what was coming. And the more important the game, the better he performed. Said Yankees left fielder Mickey Mantle, "I don't care what the situation was, how high the stakes were—the bases could be loaded and the pennant riding on every pitch, it never bothered Whitey. He pitched his game. He had nerves of steel." Ford still holds World Series career pitching records for most starts (22), wins (10), and strikeouts (94).

WHITEY FORD
PITCHER

NEW YORK
YANKEES

STATS

Yankees seasons: 1950–67

Height: 5-10

Weight: 180

- **236–106 career record**

- **.690 career winning percentage**

- **8-time All-Star**

- **Baseball Hall of Fame inductee (1974)**

its remarkable run of winning seasons. In fact, the Yanks finished above .500 every season between 1926 and 1964!

As DiMaggio's career was coming to an end in 1951, a 20-year-old rookie from Oklahoma named Mickey Mantle arrived in New York. Mantle was a switch hitter who could belt mammoth home runs from both sides of the plate. Yankees manager Casey Stengel once remarked, "There are some who say he hits with more power right-handed, and there's others who say he hits with more power left-handed. They can't make up their minds. Now, wouldn't you say that was amazing?"

PHIL RIZZUTO

A fielding dynamo, shortstop Phil Rizzuto helped the Yankees win seven World Series in the 1940s and '50s.

MICKEY MANTLE

Mantle spent one season playing right field alongside DiMaggio before taking over the prized center field spot himself. Mantle's blend of speed, power, and desire marked him as a unique talent. But he was not alone as a star in the Yankees lineup. Other Yankees greats of that era included Rizzuto, pitcher Whitey Ford, and catcher Yogi Berra—each of whom would later join Mantle in the Hall of Fame. These players helped the Yankees win eight AL pennants and seven world championships during the 1950s.

Unfortunately, Mantle's career was hampered by injuries. No one knows what records he could have set had he stayed healthy. In 1961, for example, Mantle and fellow Yankees outfielder Roger Maris excited New Yorkers and baseball fans everywhere when they began an assault on Babe Ruth's cherished record of 60 home runs in a season. As the two sluggers slammed the ball day after day, the pressure became enormous on both of them. Then Mantle was slowed by a virus and hip infection. Maris eventually broke the record on the last day of the season, while Mantle—despite his health problems—managed to finish with a career-high 54 homers. "Nobody else would have played [with injuries like Mantle's]. Nobody," said Yankees catcher Elston Howard. "But Mickey wasn't like normal people."

Mickey Mantle had epic home run power. In one 1953 game, he launched a ball that carried 565 feet.

Although often overshadowed by Mickey Mantle, Roger Maris earned lasting fame with his 61 home runs in 1961.

ROGER MARIS

THE BOSS TAKES OVER

Mantle led the Yanks to three more pennants in 1962, 1963, and 1964. Then the team and its star began to fade. Mantle retired in 1968; the AL was split into two divisions in 1969; and then the club changed players, managers, and finally, owners. In 1973, shipping magnate George Steinbrenner bought the team and began rebuilding it. Steinbrenner, whose nickname in New York was "The Boss," became famous for two things: spending money freely on talented players and criticizing his high-priced acquisitions if they didn't perform as well as he expected them to.

Among The Boss's first key moves were the signings of two free agents:

GEORGE STEINBRENNER – Baseball's most famous—and controversial—owner, Steinbrenner spent big to build the Yankees into a powerhouse. Since he took the reins in 1973, the Yankees have almost always had the highest player payroll in the majors.

CATCHER · YOGI BERRA

Today, Lawrence "Yogi" Berra is known primarily for the mind-bending comments he would occasionally make, such as, "It's tough to make predictions, especially about the future" or "It ain't over 'til it's over." But during the 1950s, Yogi was the glue that held the Yankees' dynasty together. Yogi didn't look like a great athlete. He was short and stocky, but he generated amazing power as a hitter and showed great agility as a catcher. "He seemed to be doing everything wrong, yet everything came out right," said New York Giants outfielder Mel Ott. "He stopped everything behind the plate and hit everything in front of it."

YOGI BERRA
CATCHER

NEW YORK
YANKEES

STATS

Yankees seasons: 1946–63

Height: 5-9

Weight: 195

- **1,430 career RBI**

- **3-time AL MVP**

- **15-time All-Star**

- **Baseball Hall of Fame inductee (1972)**

BUCKY DENT

THE ONE-GAME SEASON

For Yankees fans, the 1978 season was magical. That year, the Yanks made the greatest comeback in baseball history and left their archrivals, the Boston Red Sox, feeling robbed again. The Yankees had a slow and uneasy start, while the Red Sox were flying high. On July 19, New York trailed Boston in the AL East by 14 games; no team had ever made up that big of a deficit. But after contentious manager Billy Martin was fired, the Yankees calmed down under new skipper Bob Lemon and found their focus. The Yanks started winning regularly and slowly closed the gap with Boston. The clubs ended the season deadlocked at 99–63 and facing a one-game playoff in Boston's Fenway Park to decide which would advance to the postseason. Boston struck first and led 2–0 going into the seventh inning. Then the Yankees' weak-hitting shortstop, Bucky Dent, confounded everyone by lofting a three-run homer over the "Green Monster" (Fenway's left-field wall) to put the Yankees ahead. New York held on for a 5–4 win. Boston fans, who still hated the Yankees for taking Babe Ruth from them in 1920, couldn't believe the 1978 pennant had been "stolen," too.

pitcher Jim "Catfish" Hunter and slugging outfielder Reggie Jackson. These stars combined with talented players already in New York—including gritty catcher Thurman Munson, slick-fielding third baseman Graig Nettles, crafty left-handed hurler Ron Guidry, and fireballing relief pitcher Rich "Goose" Gossage—to create a rising AL power.

The atmosphere in Yankee Stadium became electric in the late 1970s as the team began to win again. The air in the clubhouse was more volatile, though, as players screamed at each other, their aggressive manager, Billy Martin, and their owner. "Some kids dream of joining the circus, others of becoming

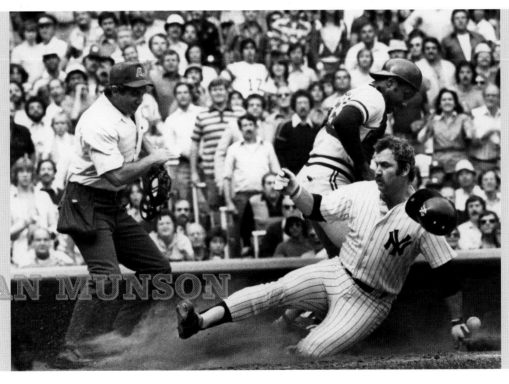

THURMAN MUNSON – The first Yankees player to be named team captain since Lou Gehrig, Munson became a seven-time All-Star by way of his brilliant defense and .292 career batting average. Tragically, he died in a plane crash at the age of 32.

a major league baseball player. As a member of the New York Yankees, I've gotten to do both," joked Nettles.

In 1976, the Yankees won their first pennant in 12 years but were swept by the Cincinnati Reds' "Big Red Machine" in the World Series. The next year, Jackson made sure they didn't lose. He pounded a record five home runs, including three in the sixth and final game of the 1977 World Series, to lead New York back to the top of the baseball world. When Jackson powered the Yanks to another championship in 1978, Steinbrenner crowned him "Mr. October," since Jackson always played his best in the postseason games of October.

After the Yankees lost the 1981 World Series, they slid downhill for the rest of the decade. The most consistent Yankees player during the 1980s was first baseman Don Mattingly, whose strong bat and remarkable fielding ability earned him the nickname "Donnie Baseball." Mattingly brought an intense attitude to the ballpark every day. "Check Donnie's eyes during a game," said Yankees pitcher Bob Tewksbury. "They're right out of a horror movie. He yells at opposing players. He paces in the dugout. I've never seen anyone compete with that kind of passion." Mattingly won the AL batting title in 1984 and was named the league's MVP in 1985. He also consistently

FIRST BASEMAN · LOU GEHRIG

Lou Gehrig once said of himself, "I'm just the guy who's in there every day, the fellow who follows Babe Ruth in the order." Yet Gehrig struck just as much fear into the hearts of AL pitchers as his more-famous teammate. He was an RBI machine, driving in 150 or more runs 7 times in his career. Gehrig earned the respect of New York fans for his courage and consistency, and when more than 61,000 turned out to honor him after he was forced to retire, the dying hero famously commented, "Today I consider myself the luckiest man on the face of the earth."

LOU GEHRIG
FIRST BASEMAN

NEW YORK
YANKEES

STATS

Yankees seasons: 1923–39

Height: 6-0

Weight: 200

- **493 career HR**

- **1,995 career RBI**

- **7-time All-Star**

- **Baseball Hall of Fame inductee (1939)**

YANKEES

"Donnie Baseball" was among the game's most complete players, despite suffering back problems late in his career.

DON MATTINGLY

SECOND BASEMAN · JOE GORDON

Joe Gordon was one of the most acrobatic second basemen of his era. He fielded balls no other infielder would even try to reach and led AL second-sackers in assists in four different seasons. Gordon was a solid, though unspectacular, hitter, but he had enough pop in his bat to set the AL record for most career home runs by a second baseman. He played in five World Series during his seven seasons with the Yankees, and he later helped lead the Cleveland Indians to their last World Series triumph in 1948.

STATS

Yankees seasons: 1938–43, 1946

Height: 5-10

Weight: 180

- **253 career HR**

- **975 career RBI**

- **1942 AL MVP**

- **9-time All-Star**

JOE GORDON
SECOND BASEMAN

NEW YORK
YANKEES

earned Gold Glove awards as the AL's top-fielding first-sacker. Unfortunately, back problems robbed him of his power and mobility during much of the last half of his career.

Despite Mattingly's fine play and that of slugging outfielder Dave Winfield, The Boss was haunted by one fact—that from 1982 to 1994, the Yanks didn't make the playoffs. "For a lot of clubs, 13 years without being in the postseason is no big deal," said Steinbrenner. "But for the New York Yankees, it is unacceptable."

Determined to build another winner, Steinbrenner took a good look at his team before the 1995 season began. His roster featured Mattingly, All-Star third baseman Wade Boggs, steady right fielder Paul O'Neill, and budding superstar Bernie Williams in center field. The Boss added strength to the mound by signing pitcher David Cone and by bringing up left-hander Andy Pettitte from the minor leagues.

The team finished second in the AL Eastern Division that season, earning the league's first-ever Wild Card berth in the playoffs. Mattingly had made it to the playoffs at last, but unfortunately, the team's 1995 postseason stay would be short; New York fell in five tight games to the Seattle Mariners in the first round. Following the season, Mattingly retired. Fans were saddened to see their hero go, but they were certain that their Yankees were ready to begin a new dynasty.

THIRD BASEMAN · GRAIG NETTLES

During his career in New York, Graig Nettles rivaled the Baltimore Orioles' Brooks Robinson as the AL's top third baseman on both defense and offense. In the field, Nettles made spectacular diving stops to turn sure doubles into outs. Then, at bat, the left-handed slugger sent balls soaring over the right-field fence in Yankee Stadium; Nettles still holds the AL career record for homers by a third-sacker. In 1977, the two-way star earned a Gold Glove award for his fielding while slamming 37 homers, driving in 107 runs, and scoring 99 runs to lead the Yankees to their first world championship in 15 years.

STATS

Yankees seasons: 1973–83

Height: 6-0

Weight: 185

- **390 career HR**
- **1,314 career RBI**
- **6-time All-Star**
- **2-time Gold Glove winner**

GRAIG NETTLES
THIRD BASEMAN

NEW YORK
YANKEES

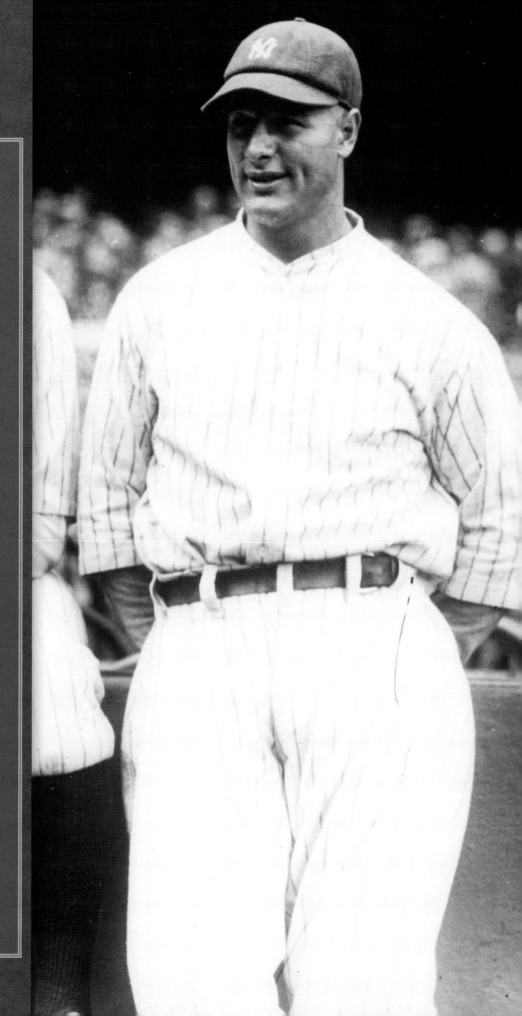

MAKING BASEBALL FASHION HISTORY

Today's professional baseball players wear colorful uniforms complete with artistic logos, numerals, and nameplates. But in baseball's earliest days, uniforms were much plainer. Then, in 1912, the Yankees decided to jazz up their bland white shirts and pants with black pinstripes. The new look thrilled fans, who felt that their players dressed classier than any other team's, even if they didn't win that often. Pinstripes have been a key part of the Yankees' look ever since. By 1929, the Yankees were the best team in baseball, and management decided to make another uniform change to show off the members of "Murderers' Row." That year, the Yanks became the first team to include permanent numbers on the backs of players' shirts. The numbers were assigned according to batting order, so because Babe Ruth and Lou Gehrig batted third and fourth, they wore numbers 3 and 4. There was no need to put the players' names on the back; fans recognized all of the Yankees' sluggers by appearance and playing style. Even today, Yankees uniforms have no names sewn on. The Yankees were also the first team to retire players' numbers, including those of Ruth, Gehrig, and 14 other immortals.

THE KID IS READY

Before the 1996 season began, Steinbrenner hired veteran manager and native New Yorker Joe Torre to assume leadership in the dugout. With his calm demeanor and vast baseball experience, Torre was the perfect choice to run the team and deal with The Boss. As one of his first moves, Torre inserted rookie shortstop Derek Jeter into the starting lineup. "The kid is ready," Torre declared. "It's time for him to earn his keep."

Jeter quickly proved that he was up to the task. The lanky, 6-foot-3 shortstop hit his first major-league homer on opening day and kept on hitting throughout the year. He finished the season with a .314 average and easily claimed AL Rookie of the Year honors. More importantly, he helped spark the Yanks to their first pennant since 1981.

Yankees fans immediately fell in love with Jeter, who combined the good looks of a movie star with the intensity and work ethic of Don Mattingly. While still in his early 20s, Jeter established himself as the club's leader on the field and in the clubhouse. (He was officially named team captain in 2003.)

The addition of Jeter and new relief ace Mariano Rivera in 1996 transformed New York from a talented team into a dominant one. In the playoffs

SHORTSTOP · DEREK JETER

When he was only five, Derek Jeter told friends that someday he would play shortstop for the New York Yankees. Sixteen years later, he was doing just that, but his baseball career didn't get off to a great start. Drafted out of high school by the Yankees in 1992, Jeter committed 56 errors in his first minor-league season. Then, with endless practice and strong determination, he made himself into a Gold Glove fielder and outstanding clutch hitter. "I work extremely hard," Jeter explained. "I like to be involved. I like to be in the middle of things, and I'm not afraid to fail."

STATS

Yankees seasons: 1995–present

Height: 6-3

Weight: 195

- .317 career BA

- 7-time All-Star

- 1996 AL Rookie of the Year

- 5 seasons of 200-plus hits

DEREK JETER
SHORTSTOP

NEW YORK
YANKEES

LEFT FIELDER · MICKEY MANTLE

Mickey Mantle was destined to become a professional baseball player. Mantle's father named him "Mickey" after his favorite ballplayer, Hall of Fame catcher Mickey Cochrane of the Detroit Tigers. Mutt Mantle also trained his son to be a switch hitter, believing this skill would give him an edge over other players. He was right; during his 18-year career in New York, Mantle batted over .300 10 times and twice topped the 50-homer mark. Although he primarily played center field, following in the footsteps of Joe DiMaggio, Mantle used his outstanding speed and defensive skills to track balls down all over the outfield.

MICKEY MANTLE
LEFT FIELDER

NEW YORK
YANKEES

STATS

Yankees seasons: 1951–68

Height: 5-11

Weight: 198

- **536 career HR**

- **3-time AL MVP**

- **16-time All-Star**

- **Baseball Hall of Fame inductee (1974)**

MARIANO RIVERA

Widely regarded as the best closer of all time, Mariano Rivera holds the big-league record for career postseason saves.

that year, the Yankees defeated the Texas Rangers and Baltimore Orioles to win the AL pennant, earning the right to battle the National League (NL) champion Atlanta Braves in the World Series. The Braves won the first two games and began dreaming of a series sweep. Then the Yanks took out their own broom, winning the next four contests to capture their first world championship in 18 years. The Yankees had given notice—they were back!

The next season, the Yanks made the playoffs again but were eliminated in the first round by the Cleveland Indians. That proved to be just a minor setback. The next three seasons, the Yankees dominated major league baseball, capturing three straight AL pennants and then winning three consecutive World Series. Yankees fans got a special thrill in 2000, when their team outdueled its crosstown rival, the New York Mets, to earn its 26th title—more than any other team in any other professional sport.

Jeter sparked the Yankees all three championship years, pounding out more than 200 hits each campaign. "Jeter gets better every year—that's what's remarkable about him," said broadcaster Ed Bradley during a profile on the TV show *60 Minutes*. "Some guys are good and stay good. Some guys are good and get better. . . . It's that way with the best, whatever the profession. That's the way this kid is."

DEREK JETER

DEREK JETER – With a career playoff batting average of .314, Jeter was the heart of the Yankees' late-1990s dynasty. His lithe profile, good looks, and classy playing style earned him comparisons to former Yankees great Joe DiMaggio.

CENTER FIELDER · JOE DiMAGGIO

"The Yankee Clipper" was more than just a great ballplayer; he was a legend. Tall, handsome, graceful, and shy, DiMaggio never seemed flustered or out of control—on or off the field. Said Yankees catcher Bill Dickey, "He was a guy who knew he was the greatest baseball player in America, and he was proud of it. He knew what the press and fans and kids expected of him, and he was always trying to live up to that image." In a nationwide poll conducted during Major League Baseball's 100th anniversary in 1969, DiMaggio easily topped the voting as the sport's "greatest living player."

JOE DiMAGGIO
CENTER FIELDER

NEW YORK
YANKEES

STATS

Yankees seasons: 1936–51

Height: 6-2

Weight: 193

- **.325 career BA**
- **3-time AL MVP**
- **13-time All-Star**
- **Baseball Hall of Fame inductee (1955)**

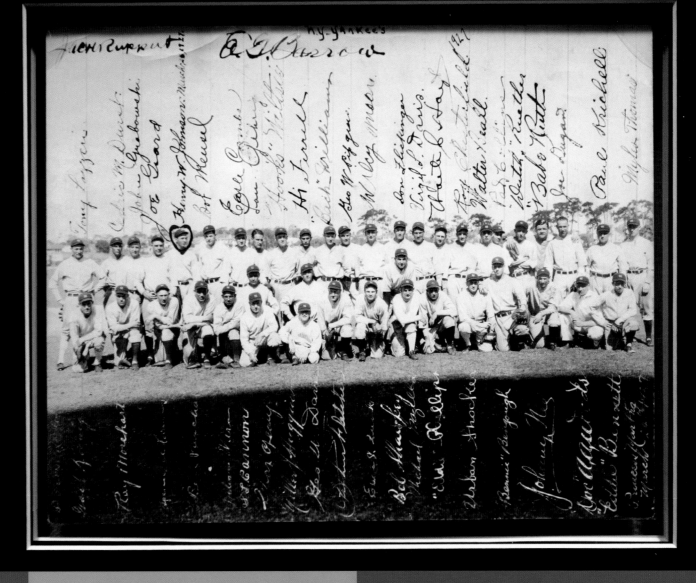

THE GREATEST TEAM EVER?

A good way to start a debate in New York is to ask a Yankees fan which was the greatest team in baseball history. Some old-time fans would argue for the 1927 Yankees, the original "Bronx Bombers" that featured Ruth and Gehrig. That club won 110 games and swept the Pittsburgh Pirates in the World Series. Other fans might name the 1961 Yanks, led by the homer-happy "M&M Boys": Mickey Mantle and Roger Maris. That club won 109 games and romped over the Cincinnati Reds in the World Series. But younger fans have their own pick—the 1998 Yankees team that featured a terrifically balanced lineup and set the AL record for most games won in a season. Led by shortstop Derek Jeter, outfielders Paul O'Neill and Bernie Williams, first baseman Tino Martinez, and pitchers David Cone, David Wells, and Mariano Rivera, the 1998 Yankees were nearly invincible. They ran off a 22–2 streak early in the season and finished the year at 114–48, 22 games ahead in the AL East. In the postseason, the Yanks won 11 more games (losing only 2), including a World Series sweep of the San Diego Padres for the 24th championship in franchise history.

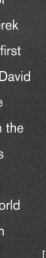

RECONSTRUCTING AN EMPIRE

The Yankees were riding high as the new millennium opened. To maintain the club's level of excellence, Steinbrenner spent big but wisely—nearly every free agent who put on the Yankees' pinstripes made major contributions on the field. Such players as pitchers Mike Mussina and Roger Clemens, outfielder Gary Sheffield, and first baseman Jason Giambi had been All-Stars with their former teams and continued to shine in New York in the early 2000s. The Yankees even reached all the way to Japan to entice outfielder Hideki Matsui to come aboard their express train.

After all the free agent signings, the Yankees' yearly payroll exceeded that of every other team in baseball. Fans in other cities complained loudly, labeling the Yankees "the best team money could buy." Fans in New York—hungry to sink their teeth into a 27th championship—dismissed such comments as mere jealousy.

The Yankees seemed on their way to that title in early September 2001. Then, on September 11, everything in New York changed when the city's World Trade Center was attacked by terrorists and nearly 3,000 people were

ALEX RODRIGUEZ

ALEX RODRIGUEZ – A natural shortstop, Rodriguez moved to third base after joining the Yankees in 2004. "A-Rod" had made history in 2000 as the highest-paid athlete of all time, signing a $252-million contract with the Texas Rangers.

RIGHT FIELDER · BABE RUTH

Excitement accompanied Babe Ruth wherever he went. "When he entered a clubhouse, a room, or a ballfield, there seemed to be flags waving and bands playing constantly," said Yankees pitcher Waite Hoyt. Ruth's appetite for food was matched only by his appetite for admiration, and his fans loved "The Sultan of Swat" after he led the AL in slugging percentage his first 13 seasons in the majors. The Babe was the highest-paid player of his era and felt he deserved every penny. When a reporter once asked Ruth why he should earn more than the president of the United States, Ruth replied, "I had a better year than he did."

BABE RUTH
RIGHT FIELDER

NEW YORK
YANKEES

STATS

Yankees seasons: 1920–34

Height: 6-2

Weight: 215

- **714 career HR**

- **2,217 career RBI**

- **.342 career BA**

- **Baseball Hall of Fame inductee (1936)**

killed. Baseball was put on hold for several weeks while the city and the country attempted to recover. When play resumed, so did the Yankees' pennant drive. They won the AL East again, then they knocked off the Oakland A's and Seattle Mariners in the playoffs to earn a berth in the World Series against the Arizona Diamondbacks.

In one of the most exciting and emotional World Series of all time, the two teams battled through seven tense contests. In the bottom of the ninth inning of Game 7, the Yankees held a 2–1 lead, and closer Mariano Rivera was on the mound in Arizona's Bank One Ballpark. Throughout the Yanks' successful run of the late '90s, Rivera had been consistently excellent. Many baseball experts considered him the greatest relief pitcher of all time, particularly when the pressure was on in the postseason. But this time, Rivera ran out of gas. Arizona scored twice to win the game and the series, four games to three.

If fans doubted the Yankees' ability to make a comeback, they were reassured as the club continued its mastery of the AL East by capturing five straight division titles between 2002 and 2006. The Yankees faltered in the playoffs, however, reaching the World Series only once (in 2003). That time, a young expansion team, the Florida Marlins, was ready for the Yanks, winning the second championship in its brief history and preventing New York from wearing a 27th crown.

The Yankees then regrouped and began constructing what Steinbrenner

MANAGER · JOE TORRE

When Joe Torre was first named manager of the Yankees, many New York fans were unhappy. Torre had previously managed in St. Louis, Atlanta, and New York (with the Mets) and had had limited success. But the Brooklyn native quickly changed fans' opinions by winning a world championship in his first year at the helm. At the ticker-tape parade that followed the big win, Torre commented, "Maybe the Good Lord was just waiting for me to put on the pinstripes." In Torre's years piloting the Yankees, his clubs won more than 1,000 games and reached the playoffs every year.

STATS

Yankees seasons as manager: 1996–present

Height: 6-2

Weight: 210

Managerial Record: 1,973–1,702

World Series Championships: 1996, 1998, 1999, 2000

JOE TORRE
MANAGER

NEW YORK
YANKEES

TINO MARTINEZ

EXTRAORDINARY ENDINGS

The 2001 World Series between the Yankees and Arizona Diamondbacks featured some eerie events. The Diamondbacks started quickly, winning Games 1 and 2 at home behind pitching aces Curt Schilling and Randy Johnson. The teams went to New York for Game 3, and emotions ran high. Fans cheered and cried as a flag that had flown at the World Trade Center on September 11 was displayed, and the Yanks managed a narrow 2–1 victory. In Game 4, which took place on Halloween, the Diamondbacks led 3–1 with two outs in the ninth before Yankees first baseman Tino Martinez hit a two-run homer off Arizona reliever Byung-Hyun Kim to tie the contest. One inning later, as the clock struck midnight, Derek Jeter homered to give the Yankees the win. Most Yankees fans believed that comeback would never be equaled. But, incredibly, the same thing happened the next night; this time, third baseman Scott Brosius hit a game-tying homer off Kim in the ninth, and the Yankees won in extra innings again. The magic ended when the teams returned to Arizona. Johnson dominated New York's batters in Game 6, and the Diamondbacks staged their own dramatic comeback to win Game 7 and claim the championship.

YANKEES

hoped would be an even better team. Management engineered trades for two of the best players in all of baseball—pitcher Randy Johnson, winner of four Cy Young Awards as the league's best pitcher, and third baseman Alex Rodriguez, the 2003 AL MVP—putting them alongside such stars as Jeter and slugging designated hitter Jason Giambi. With these talented players, the team won the division in 2004, 2005, and 2006 (posting the best record in baseball that season), but play stopped there.

Despite the disappointing finish to the 2006 season, Yankees fans were encouraged by the young talent coming up from the club's minor-league system. Second baseman Robinson Cano showed star potential with his quick bat and good range in the field, and rookie right-hander Chien-Ming Wang, a native of Taiwan, emerged as a key man in the club's pitching rotation with a 19–6 record in 2006.

Over the past 100 years, the New York Yankees have spoiled their fans with their consistently outstanding play. Because the team has won so often and the caliber of play has been so great, Yankees fans expect every year to end with a championship. One advertising slogan used by club management in the early 2000s invited fans to "come to Yankee Stadium and see baseball history being made." No baseball team has had a more glorious history than the New York Yankees, and no team is more confident that its future will continue to be bright.

Sweet-swinging second baseman Robinson Cano emerged as an All-Star in 2006, the Yankees' 104th season.

INDEX